# THE SECRET WORLD OF

# Bears

# THE SECRET WORLD OF
# Bears

Rod Preston-Mafham

## www.raintreepublishers.co.uk
Visit our website to find out more information about **Raintree** books.

To order:
 Phone 44 (0) 1865 888112
 Send a fax to 44 (0) 1865 314091
 Visit the Raintree Bookshop at www.raintreepublishers.co.uk to browse our catalogue and order online.

First published in Great Britain by Raintree,
Halley Court, Jordan Hill, Oxford
OX2 8EJ, part of Harcourt Education.
Raintree is a registered trademark of Harcourt Education Ltd.

Text © Harcourt Education Ltd 2003
The moral right of the proprietor has been asserted.

Produced for Raintree by Discovery Books
Editors: Helen Dwyer and Catherine Clarke
Series Consultant: Michael Chinery
Design: Ian Winton
Illustrations: Stuart Lafford
Production: Jonathan Smith

Originated by Dot Gradations Ltd
Printed and bound in China by South China Printing Company

ISBN 1 844 21588 1
07 06 05 04 03
10 9 8 7 6 5 4 3 2 1

**British Library Cataloguing in Publication Data**
Preston-Mafham, Rod
The Secret World of Bears
599.7'8
A full catalogue record for this book is available from the British Library.

**Acknowledgements**
The publishers would like to thank the following for permission to reproduce photographs:
Ancient Art & Architecture p. **12**; Bruce Coleman Collection pp. **9** (John Shaw), **14 & 15** (Jorg & Petra Wegner), **17** (Johnny Johnson), **20** (Rod Williams), **25** (Jorg & Petra Wegner), **26 & 34** (Hans Reinhard), **35 & 37** (Dr. Eckart Pott); Natural History Photographic Agency pp. **8** (Andy Rouse), **13** (Daniel Heuclin/Musee Lecoq), **16** (Andy Rouse), **18** (Rich Kirchner), **22/23 & 24** (T Kitchin & V Hurst), **29** ( James Warwick), **31** (Gerard Lacz), **32** (Andy Rouse), **33** (David E Myers), **38** (Kevin Schafer), **39** (B & C Alexander), **40** (Kevin Schafer), **41** (Andy Rouse), **42** (David Middleton); Oxford Scientific Films pp. **11** (Konrad Wothe), **19** (Dan Gurarich), **21** (Mike Hill), **27** (Dan Gurarich), **30** (Daniel J Cox), **36-37** (Konrad Wothe),
All background images © Steck-Vaughn Collection (Corbis Royalty Free, Getty Royalty Free, and StockBYTE).

Cover photograph reproduced with permission of the Natural History Photographic Agency (John Shaw).

Any words appearing in the text in bold, **like this**, are explained in the Glossary.

# Contents

# What is a bear?

A teddy bear may be a cuddly toy, but real bears are very dangerous animals. Bears are carnivorous, which means they belong to the group of **mammals** that feed on meat – that is, on other animals. Other **carnivores** include cats, dogs, otters and badgers. These mammals all look and behave quite differently, but what they nearly all

Bears are found in both North and South America, in Europe and throughout much of Asia. They are not native to Africa, Australia or Antarctica.

There are around 240 species of carnivores in the world today, and only 8 of these are bears.

The closest relations of the bear are the members of the dog, raccoon and weasel families.

The polar bear is the largest land-based carnivore alive today.

**thick fur**
For protection and warmth. Grows thicker for the winter.

▶ Bears are very heavily built animals with a large head. They have strong jaws, quite short legs and big feet with long, sharp claws. Bears also have a large nose and a very good sense of smell, which helps them to find food and sense possible danger.

have in common are two pairs of scissor-like back teeth, known as **carnassials**, that can slice through the flesh of their **prey**.

## THE BEAR FACTS

There are eight **species** of bear. They range in size from the enormous polar bear, weighing around 600 kilograms, to the tiny sun bear that weighs only 65 kilograms. Despite these size differences, all bears have the same general appearance. All are heavily built animals with quite short legs and very short tails. The head is large, and in most species the **muzzle** is long. A bear's lips are not attached to its gums, so the lips move easily and can be stuck out. Bears have small ears and eyes so they cannot hear or see all that well, but they have a big nose and a great sense of smell.

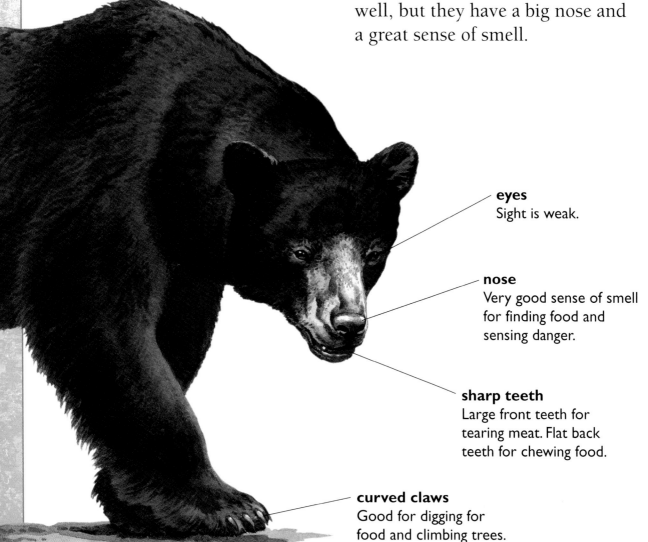

**eyes**
Sight is weak.

**nose**
Very good sense of smell for finding food and sensing danger.

**sharp teeth**
Large front teeth for tearing meat. Flat back teeth for chewing food.

**curved claws**
Good for digging for food and climbing trees.

## WHERE BEARS LIVE

Most bears live in the cooler parts of the world, although the sun bear lives in the **tropics**. Bears live mostly in forested areas where there is some space between the trees. Open forest provides them with the variety of plants and animals on which they feed. The only bear that does not live in forests is, of course, the polar bear, which lives on the Arctic ice sheets.

Brown bears live in the northern parts of North America, Europe and Asia. Grizzly bears, like this one, are at home in the snow-covered forests of Canada.

One group of North American black bears lives in the forests of the Okefenokee swamp on the borders of Georgia and Florida in the USA. Here they live quite happily, despite the fact that much of the area is flooded throughout the year.

Bears walk with their feet flat and their heels touching the ground. The soles of their feet are often hairy. Polar bears, in particular, need furry-soled feet to keep them from slipping on the smooth ice. Those **species** that climb trees, such as the black bear and the sloth bear, have hairless soles to their feet. Their foot pads have a rough surface that enables them to grip. Bears have wide, powerful paws with tough, thick claws for grasping food, digging and defending their young.

Bears normally walk on all fours, but they can stand and walk on their back legs – although rather clumsily. Standing up helps them look out for danger or **prey**, which is important because their eyesight is poor. It also allows them to reach up to pick fruits and berries from trees.

# Not a bear!

Many people think that the koala is a type of bear. In the past it was often called the 'koala bear', probably because of its bear-like appearance. In fact, the koala is not related to the bear. It is a marsupial (a mammal with a pouch), found only in Australia.

# The origin of bears

Around the time that dinosaurs died out, about 65 million years ago, carnivores first appeared. Today there are two main groups of carnivores. The cats and their relations are in one group, and bears are in the other, along with dogs, raccoons and weasels.

True bears appeared on Earth about 20 million years ago.

Although bears are called carnivores, much of their diet consists of plants.

The first known bear-like animals lived on Earth about 34 million years ago. These creatures were about the size of foxes and lived in the forests of Asia, where they probably hunted in trees. After this early **ancestor** of the bears, the next oldest **fossils** we know about date from about 20 million years ago. These were of an animal that was definitely a bear. This creature is thought of as the ancestor of all of today's modern bears. Known as the dawn bear, it was about 75 centimetres high at the shoulder. Like its ancestors, it probably spent a lot of its time in the trees.

### EARLY BEARS

The first pandas also appeared about 20 million years ago. Fossils of several different **species** of early panda have been found. The oldest fossils of the present-day panda, however, are only 3 million years old. All known panda fossils have been discovered in China.

The ancestors of the spectacled bear are the next oldest species. They first appeared between 10 and 15 million years ago. These bears moved out of forests into more open areas with fewer trees, and became fast-running hunters.

Many species of this running bear **evolved** during the next few million years, especially in the Americas. Some of them, including the huge Florida cave bear, stopped eating meat altogether. Most of the running bear species had died out by about 10,000 years ago, although the Florida cave bear may still have been around 8000 years ago. The only living member of this group is the spectacled bear of South America, which has given up running and now lives mainly in the forests.

The earliest bears probably lived in the trees, and a few modern bears are still good climbers. Most bear species, such as this brown bear, are now too big to climb high up into the trees.

## URSINE BEARS

The other six **species** of bear alive today are usually called the **ursine** (bear-like) bears. They are given this name because they are more **typical** bears. The first of the ursine bears was the little bear, which appeared 5 or 6 million years ago. It was a small bear, with scissor-like back teeth – showing that it was very much a meat-eater. Scientists believe that the little bear was the **ancestor** of the six types of living ursine bears and also of many **extinct** species known only from **fossils**.

A carving of a bear in stone that was made in Germany sometime between 15,000 and 10,000 B.C. Carvings of bears, made by ancient peoples, have been discovered in many different parts of the world.

Some of these extinct bears were very large. They included the European cave bear, which was closely related to today's European brown bear but about three times as big. This large bear lived up until about 10,000 years ago. It was well known to humans, who left paintings of the animals they had seen on the walls of their caves.

These cave paintings show that bears were hunted by early humans. These people would not only have eaten bear meat, but also used their skins and bones too. In cold periods, when ice covered much of the ground, bear skins would have made warm clothing and perhaps tent-like shelters. The bones could be made into weapons and tools such as needles.

# Cave bear finds

The massive European cave bear was the most powerful **carnivore** of its time in Europe and Asia. Its bones have been found in caves all over Europe. Bears would **hibernate** in caves and often died during the winter. In caves the bones were well-protected from the weather and **scavengers**, which is why so many caves contain huge quantities of bones. In one cave alone, 30,000 bones were found. This skull of a cave bear was found in a cave in France.

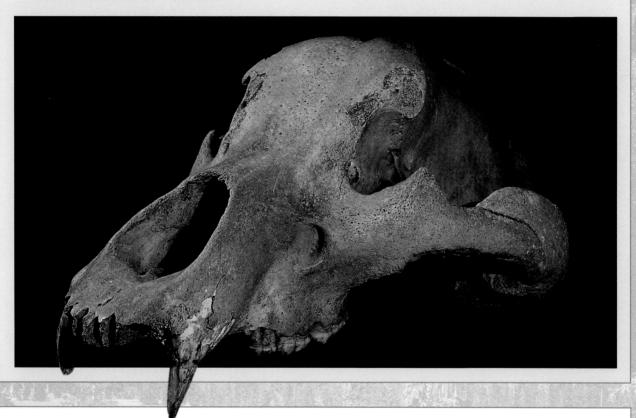

### VEGETARIAN TEETH

Although the cave bears and some of the other bears that **evolved** from the little bear became very large, they gradually turned from meat-eating to a more **omnivorous** diet, rather like our own, with lots of plant matter. Along with this change of diet, their teeth began to change. The scissor-like **carnassial** teeth, used for slicing through flesh, gradually became less sharp and the surfaces of all the teeth in the cheeks became flatter and more suitable for grinding up plant food.

# Bears today

Fully grown male bears are always larger than females of the same species.

The largest of the bears that spend all their time on land is the Kodiak bear, a type of brown bear that can weigh up to 680 kilograms.

When standing up, the tallest bear is the polar bear, which can reach 3 metres in height. At the other end of the scale, the sun bear measures around 1.25 metres when upright.

The giant panda has an extra 'thumb' on each hand. Often called the sixth claw, it is not a real thumb, but it can move like one. It helps the animal to grasp the bamboo stems on which it feeds. It is formed from one of the wrist bones and is covered with a rough, thick pad.

## GIANT PANDAS

With its thick, woolly, black and white fur, and black eyes and ears, the giant panda cannot be mistaken for any other bear. It is one of the smallest bears, with a maximum male weight of about 150 kilograms and a height of about 1.5 metres. When it was first discovered, scientists thought it was related either to the raccoon or the much smaller red panda. More recently, studies of the giant

In Wolong Reserve in south-west China, this panda bear digs into a meal of bamboo, its main source of food in the wild.

panda's body show that it is much more closely related to the bear family. The giant panda was once found in many places in China, but much of its **habitat** – bamboo forest – has been destroyed and the giant panda now remains in only a few remote forests in south-west China.

## SPECTACLED BEARS

A spectacled bear is usually dark brown in colour, with lighter fur around the eyes. This makes it look like it is wearing spectacles!

The spectacled bear is the only **species** in South America, where it is found mainly in the Andes mountains of Venezuela, Colombia, Peru, Bolivia and Ecuador. It lives mostly in forests, but is sometimes found even higher up the mountains in the cold grasslands where trees cannot survive. Male spectacled bears can

Spectacled bears are so called because of the light markings found around the eyes. These markings can vary greatly from bear to bear.

get quite large, weighing up to 200 kilograms and standing up to 2.1 metres tall.

15

## POLAR BEARS

The largest and most easily recognized of the **ursine** bears is the polar bear, which lives in the cold Arctic regions. The polar bear **evolved** into its present form only about 2 million years ago. Scientists believe that its **ancestors** were a population of large brown bears that had not completely given up eating meat. The fact that polar bears and brown bears can **mate** with each other and produce young shows that they are very closely related **species**.

The huge polar bear is covered with thick, **water-resistant** white fur on top of a black skin. It has an excellent sense of smell and can bound across the ice at great speed. It spends much of its life hunting for food in the icy waters of the Arctic Ocean. Polar bears have been found swimming many kilometres from the nearest land. A 10-centimetre-thick layer of fat, or blubber, under the skin allows the polar bear to keep warm even in the coldest conditions.

Because they have poor eyesight, bears rely heavily on their sense of smell to find food. This polar bear, in Arctic Norway, stands on its back legs and sniffs the air, perhaps trying to pick up the scent of a seal.

## BROWN BEARS

Brown bears, also known as grizzly bears in the USA, live in the Rockies and the Pacific North-west of North America, in parts of Europe and throughout much of the northern part of Asia. Although they are called brown bears, they can in fact be almost any colour between black and pale cream. In the Pamir and Tien Shan Mountains of Central Asia, some of the cream-coloured bears also have pale claws instead of dark brown ones. These pale bears have been given the name of Isabelline, or white-clawed, bears. It was once thought that there were many species of brown bear, but we now know that they all belong to a single, very changeable species.

## KODIAK BEARS

The largest brown bears are the Kodiak bears that live on the Kodiak island of Alaska. The males can weigh as much as 680 kilograms. At the other end of the scale, the brown bears living in the Spanish Pyrenees weigh less than 200 kilograms.

The grizzly bear, the North American form of the brown bear, usually lives alone. These three, however, are in the McNeil River Bear Sanctuary in Alaska, where they have come together to feed on the salmon swimming upstream to **spawn**.

## BLACK BEARS

The American black bear is found over much of the USA and Canada. This bear is usually black, with a paler **muzzle**, but it can also be brown, reddish-brown, or blueish-black. So how do you tell a brown bear from a black bear? In general, black bears are smaller than brown bears. Brown bears also have a hump at the shoulders and are more aggressive than black bears. Black bears are skilful tree climbers, but the heavier brown bears are not.

The Asian black bear can be found in various places on the continent of Asia, including northern India and Nepal, parts of Cambodia, China, Laos, Thailand, Vietnam and some Japanese islands. It is also found in the very far east of Russia, in the forest of the region called Ussuriland, which

Despite their large size, American black bears are good climbers. They climb trees to find food and to escape from danger. The long, sharp claws **typical** of bears can be seen quite clearly on the front paws of this bear.

# High-speed bears

Bears may look slow and clumsy, but they can actually run very fast. The American black bear can run at speeds of up to 40 kilometres (25 miles) an hour when chasing **prey**. Even faster are polar bears, which can reach up to 56 kilometres (35 miles) an hour. This is fast enough to chase and catch a running reindeer, and they can easily outrun a human. However, bears can only run at these high speeds for a few minutes. Their thick fur and blubber (fat) make them too hot. Polar bears can also swim at up to 10 kilometres (6 miles) an hour.

borders China and Korea. The Asian black bear is roughly the same size as the American black bear but has noticeably bigger ears and a band of pale fur across its chest. Although it is called a black bear, in some areas its shaggy coat is more brown in colour. The Asian black bear is also an excellent tree climber.

Studies of these bears in the wild have found that they live for a very long time, on average for 25 years.

## SLOTH BEARS

The sloth bear and the sun bear are both small, **nocturnal** bears. The sloth bear is found mainly in Sri Lanka and India. Its long, shaggy black hair and pale **muzzle** and chest patch make it easy to identify. Although small compared to other bears, males can still weigh as much as 135 kilograms and stand up to 1.9 metres tall. The sloth bear is an expert climber and, with the aid of its big claws, can hang upside-down from the branches like a sloth (a large, South American **mammal** that lives in trees). Although normally nocturnal, female sloth bears with cubs may sometimes come out during the day. This may be because they are trying to protect their cubs from **predators**, which come out at night to hunt.

## SUN BEARS

The smallest of all bears, the sun bear, is also black. It has very small ears and short fur – suited to its life in the hot **tropics**. It has a grey muzzle and a pale-coloured patch on its chest, which varies a lot

Despite its long, shaggy hair, the sloth bear is usually found in the tropics. The sloth bear lives mainly on insects, but it also enjoys fruit, eggs and honey. This one lives in India.

from bear to bear. This patch often spreads across the chest in a clear U-shape, but in some bears it is so small it is hard to see. This bear lives in the forests of Vietnam, Laos, Cambodia, Thailand, Burma, Malaysia, Borneo and Sumatra.

The sun bear is the world's smallest bear, measuring about 1.25 metres from head to tail. It is easy to identify from the pale, U-shaped mark across its chest.

# Food and feeding

Although bears are **carnivores**, they are known to eat almost anything. Many are **omnivorous**, which means they will eat a mixture of meat and plants. Their teeth show how they have **evolved**, or changed, to cope with this mixed diet. All bears have pointed **canine** teeth, like those of a cat or dog, that are used to grip and hold on to their **prey**. They also have wide, flat **molars**, similar to those of humans, that are suited to chewing up plants.

Bears are always on the lookout for something to eat. Black bears use their powerful claws to tear their way into bees' nests so they can feed on the grubs and honey inside. Their thick fur protects them from the stings of the angry bees.

**The polar bear is the only bear species in the world today that eats mainly meat. It is, therefore, the only bear with well-developed, slicing, carnassial teeth.**

**The spectacled bear is very fond of fruit and is a good climber. It plays an important role in the forest by spreading the seeds of the trees from which it feeds.**

**Sloth bears dig holes in termite mounds, blow away the loose dust, and then suck the termites into their mouth, like a vacuum cleaner.**

**The polar bear has a huge stomach. It can eat as much as one-fifth of its body weight at a single meal.**

## Omnivorous diets

The brown bear, the black bear, the sun bear and the spectacled bear will eat almost anything that they come across as long as it is not harmful. Leaves, fruits and berries make up about 80 per cent of the brown bear's diet. The rest is made up of live or dead animals including insects, worms, fish, small **mammals** and, sometimes, larger mammals such as deer.

Bears' diets change with the seasons. For example, they eat young plant shoots and leaves in spring and fruits and berries in autumn. This grizzly bear is feasting on a patch of blueberries in the Denali **National Park**, Alaska.

Brown bears can adapt or change their diet if they have to. When meat, including fish, is available, brown bears will catch and eat it, but in areas where there is little meat they eat more plants.

## FRUIT AND NUTS

Black bears feed in a similar way to brown bears. What they eat varies with where they are and with the season. Spring time provides them with buds and fresh young leaves, while autumn brings large amounts of all kinds of fruit on which they can fatten themselves up before winter.

The spectacled bear feeds mainly on fruit and has jaws strong

An American black bear in the Rocky Mountains enjoys the berries on a rowan tree in winter. Being able to stand on two legs is a great help when a bear is reaching for fruit.

enough to break open tough nuts. Like the other bears, however, spectacled bears will eat any animals that they can catch or kill, and they do not mind eating carrion (dead animals).

Less is known about the diet of the sun bear. It uses its long tongue to pull all kinds of insects, especially **termites**, out from their hiding places. The sun bear can be a nuisance on fruit farms, where it feeds on the young buds of bananas and coconut palms.

The sun bear is a very good climber and some scientists think that it sleeps up in the trees. Sadly, sun bear cubs are sometimes taken as pets by local people. However, sun bears can be aggressive, and by 4–5 years of age they can no longer be trusted not to attack. So they are either killed or released back into the wild. Without knowing how to search for food, their chances of survival are not very good.

Like most bears, the sun bear feeds on a mixture of plants and animals. Its very long tongue helps it to pull termites and other insects and their grubs out from the places where they hide.

## HUNTING AND FISHING

The two largest types of bear, the brown bear and the polar bear, have a diet that is rich in meat. The grizzly bears of North America and Siberia seem to enjoy fishing for salmon when the fish are swimming up the rivers to **spawn**. The grizzlies get together, often in large numbers, in areas where the rivers are quite shallow and the fish are easier to catch. Here, they fill up on the very nutritious (energy giving) salmon. Older, more experienced bears pick the best spots for fishing and drive off any other bear that tries to fish there. Young bears try desperately to grab hold of the slippery fish. By watching the older bears, the young bears soon learn how and where to fish.

A brown bear reaches out, jaws wide open, to catch a salmon as it jumps up a waterfall on its way upstream to its spawning site. During the spawning season, fish are a very important part of the bear's diet.

## POLAR BEAR DIET

The polar bear eats mainly meat. During the winter months it catches ringed seals by waiting next to the holes in the ice where the seals come up to breathe. When a seal appears, the bear grabs it with a huge paw and throws it up on to the ice. Polar bears also go hunting, often travelling as much as 80 kilometres (50 miles) a day across ice floes (floating lumps of ice) in search of seals.

## SUMMER HUNTING

Most animals eat well in the summer months in order to fatten up for the winter, when less food is available. The polar bear does the opposite. In the Arctic, there is

Polar bears eat more meat than any other type of bear. This young bear has caught a ringed seal, its main **prey**. First it eats the outer layers of skin and fatty blubber and then, if it is really hungry, it eats the red meat.

plenty of food available in the winter, but polar bears have a difficult time hunting in the summer when the sea ice melts. In the summer, they depend on stored body fat and **scavenge** anything else they can. Fruit is part of their diet at this time, as well as seabirds and their eggs and young. In summer, some towns in Alaska and northern Canada have problems with polar bears that come into town to raid rubbish dumps. This can be dangerous for the people who live there.

## SPECIAL DIETS

Although the giant panda has given up the **carnivorous** diet of its **ancestors**, its body still does not process plant material very well. The giant panda has to eat a lot of bamboo – perhaps 9 kilograms each day – in order to get enough nourishment (energy) from it. Apart from an occasional small, mouse-like **mammal** and a few insects, it does not eat meat. This could be because there are very few animals the slow-moving panda could catch, even if it wanted to.

## ANT EATER

Another special feeder is the sloth bear, with a diet made up mainly of ants and **termites**. It has long claws and powerful front teeth for breaking logs and getting to insects and other minibeasts. Its long, sticky tongue mops up its insect food easily. Alternatively, having made a hole in a termite mound, the sloth bear blows out any dust and then sucks up the termites like a vacuum cleaner. While it is sucking up termites, the sloth bear makes a strange noise.

Sloth bears use their enormous strength and long claws to tear open termite mounds to get at the grubs and termites inside. This is not as easy to do as you may think. Termites cement their nest mound together as they build it so it is almost as hard as rock.

## Placid pandas

Because pandas get very little energy from their food they are not very active animals and spend a lot of time sitting around, doing nothing in particular. Most of their life is spent moving from one patch of food to another, eating, resting and then moving on to the next patch of food. If pandas were any more active, they would run out of energy and might die.

It is said that this noise is so loud it can be heard from a distance of 100 metres or more. Getting at their termite food and sucking it up stirs up a lot of dust. The bears are able to close their nostrils to stop the dust from getting up their noses.

Few other animals eat termites in the places where the sloth bear lives. This means that sloth bears can find good supplies of termites throughout the year. The sloth bear will also eat fruit when it is in season, as well as flowers, grass, eggs and honey.

# Reproduction

Bears like to live alone. They look for each other's company only when males and females are ready to **mate**. A female bear will leave scent marks as she moves about looking for food. These let wandering male bears know that she is around. Once a male bear has found a female, he may visit her over a period of several days until she is finally ready to mate with him. Polar bear couples will stay together for a few days and mate more than once. In some places, groups of polar bears gather at mating time. There, males may mate with more than one female and females with more than one male.

Although bears live alone for most of their adult lives, males and females have to get together in order to produce young. Here, a male Alaskan brown bear approaches a female in the hope that she will allow him to mate with her.

Bears begin reproducing at between 3 and 6 years of age depending on the species.

Although they start reproducing at a younger age, male polar bears and Alaskan brown bears reach their full size only when they are about 11 years old.

Newborn bear cubs are very small, compared to their mothers. The female panda is 800 times heavier than her newborn cubs. In comparison, human mothers are about 15 times heavier than their newborn babies.

Bears produce a milk that is very rich in fat, so their cubs grow fast once they are born. Polar bear milk contains as much as 40 per cent fat, compared with about 4 or 5 per cent in cows' milk.

## GIVING BIRTH

For bears, the gestation period – the time during which the cubs develop inside their mothers – ranges from 16 to 39 weeks. Big bears take longer to develop than small bears. Most bears produce one or two cubs, but sometimes up to four may be born. The mother gives birth in the safety of a **den**. Polar bear cubs are born in the middle of winter, in a den dug deep into a snowdrift. The newborn cubs are blind, helpless and usually have no fur. Panda, polar bear and spectacled bear cubs, however, do have a thin layer of fur when they are born.

Like most **mammals**, female bears are very caring mothers and spend a great deal of time looking after their young. Here, a brown bear cub is licking its mother's nose, perhaps letting her know it's hungry.

## BEAR CUBS

The cubs stay with their mother in the **den** for the first few weeks of their lives. During this time, the female does not go out to feed but keeps herself busy with **grooming**, cleaning and feeding her cubs.

The young cubs do not have very much fur at first and so she must stay with them to keep them warm, like a bird sitting with its chicks in the nest. She keeps the den clean and tidy until they are all ready to

A mother polar bear and her two cubs outside the den in which the cubs were born. Perhaps this is the cubs' first sight of the world of ice and snow in which they will spend the rest of their lives.

leave. By then, the mother may have lost one-third of her weight because she has not been out of the den to feed, having stayed with her cubs.

Eventually, mother and cubs leave the den so that she can hunt for food. The cubs follow their mother around, learning from her what can be eaten and how to catch their own food. One thing that the mother bear has to do, which may seem strange to us, is to keep her cubs away from male bears. It is quite common for a male bear to kill young cubs. A female bear will actively defend her cubs against males, even though they are usually much bigger than her. Many cubs are quite good at climbing trees, and their mother will often send them up a tree to keep them safe while she chases off males.

Once they are large enough to look after themselves, the cubs are left to make their own way in the world by their mother as she goes off on her own.

## Follow the leader

Once they leave the den in which they were born, it is normal for bear cubs to follow their mother around until they can look after themselves. Most bear cubs walk beside their mother, but a female sloth bear allows her cubs to ride around on her back.

# Bear behaviour

Bears are big and need a lot to eat. This is one of the reasons why they prefer to live alone. If too many bears lived in one place, food would soon run out, leading to fighting and probably the death of the weaker bears. Most bears have no real enemies, apart from humans. This means they can mostly look after themselves and do not need the protection offered by a group.

Male bears will often stand on their back legs to make themselves look bigger when they are competing with other males for a female.

Like most mammals, young bears spend a lot of time playing with one another. This teaches them some of the behaviour patterns that they will need when they are grown up.

Lone bears have been seen 'playing' on their own. In particular, both American black bears and pandas sometimes slide down snowy slopes, as if they were sledging!

A male Kodiak brown bear threatening another male, who is out of view of the camera. This aggressive behaviour is normally only seen during the **mating** season, when two or more males are competing for a single female.

## BEAR TALK

Unlike their close relatives in the dog family, bears are quiet creatures. However, they do produce a number of sounds, which seem to have particular meanings. In general, it seems that the greatest amount of 'talking' takes place among bears that live in forests, where keeping track of one another among the trees is difficult. Polar bears, living on the open ice, can see each other clearly and so hardly 'talk' with one another at all.

One of the most common sounds, the roar, is produced by all bears. It means that the animal is feeling angry, and it acts as a warning to others to stay out of its way. Female bears produce sounds to keep in contact with their cubs.

Play is important in helping young mammals learn some of the skills that they will need later in adult life. These two young brown bears seem to be tussling over a tree branch.

The cubs, in turn, make sounds that the mother understands. Both spectacled and sloth bear cubs have been heard to squeal or yelp when they are in trouble.

## PLAYING

Like most baby **mammals**, bear cubs play with each other a great deal. During this play, they are practising the kinds of things they will have to do when they leave their mother: search for food, kill **prey**, run from danger and how to behave when they meet other bears. Play-fighting is very common, even in almost fully grown cubs, but the bears stop before they hurt one another.

## WINTER SLEEP

Whether a bear sleeps through most of the winter depends upon its food supply. Pandas and spectacled, sloth and sun bears, which all live in warm places, have food available throughout the year and do not sleep through winter. Polar bears do best during the winter when their main food – seals – is widely available. They do slow down a bit in summer, but do not sleep through it.

Black bears and brown bears are the two **species** that sleep for part of the winter. The further north a bear lives, the longer it sleeps. Brown bears living in the far north of North America, for example, can sleep for as long as seven months of the year.

Spring has arrived, the snow is beginning to melt, and this brown bear is now emerging from its winter den.

American black bears further south may sleep for as little as two weeks. The bears fatten themselves up during autumn so that they have enough food stored in their bodies to keep them going through the winter. Brown bears often dig their own **dens** in the sides of hills, or use piles of brushwood (broken twigs) or logs. American black bears prefer hollow trees, but they too will use brushwood or even small caves.

Snug in their den, a mother bear and her half-grown cubs sleep away the freezing days of winter. Moving around through the deep snow would be difficult, and not much food is available at this time of year.

The bears' winter sleep is sometimes called **hibernation**, but it is not nearly such a deep sleep as that of other animals that hibernate, such as the dormouse or hedgehog. The body temperature of these animals drops to near freezing, and their bodies slow almost to a stop. This is true hibernation and the animals take a long time to wake up from it. The temperature of sleeping bears, however, drops by only a few degrees and the animals take only a few minutes to wake up.

# Keeping cool

The thick layer of fat that keeps polar bears warm in the icy Arctic waters is a problem for them in summer. It makes it very difficult for them to keep cool. One way they solve this problem is by lying down on the remaining patches of ice or by spending more time in the water.

# Bears and people

The panda – the bear that is the easiest to recognize – has been chosen as the emblem of the World Wide Fund for Nature (WWF), an organization that works to protect wildlife. Although the panda has become a symbol of **conservation**, it is **endangered**, as are five other bear **species**. Only the polar bear, brown bear and American black bear are, at the moment, reasonably safe from **extinction**.

The earliest known examples of cave drawings of bears are thought to be about 35,000 years old.

Six states in the USA have a bear as their emblem. The grizzly bear is the official state animal of California.

About 6000 European brown bears live in the mountain forests of Transylvania, in Romania, where they are protected by law.

In the past, bears have not been treated very kindly by humans, and things are not much better today. In Poland, Romania and Russia, bears are still taught to dance and perform other tricks.

An organization called 'Libearty' was formed in 1992. Its aim is to protect bears around the world from cruel treatment by humans.

This captive sloth bear is used by its handler in India to entertain tourists. Sloth bears are an endangered species.

Humans and bears have come into contact with each other for thousands of years. The fondness we have for bears may be due to the fact that, like us, they often stand up and walk on their back legs. From a distance, they can even look like a human being. In the past, some humans, especially Native Americans, may have **worshipped** bears.

The Inuit people, in the far north of North America, have had a long history of living with the polar bear. Taking great care – because polar bears are dangerous animals – the Inuit still hunt bears for both meat and skins. Skins are the best material for making warm, snow-proof trousers. The Inuit still admire and respect these animals, and many still think of polar bear hunting as a test of bravery.

The native peoples of the Arctic regions have a long history of hunting polar bears for their skins and meat and still do so sometimes. Here, polar bear skins are hung out to dry in north-western Greenland.

A cuddly teddy bear is often a child's first toy. This friendly and loveable image of bears appears in characters from children's books, films and television. In real life, however, bears are not friendly towards humans and can be very dangerous. Most dangerous of all is a female bear with cubs that she feels are in danger.

## PROBLEM BEARS

As the number of humans on Earth increases, human contact with bears also increases. Humans are settling in ever more **remote** places, where they are invading and often destroying the **habitats** in which bears live.

In North America, for example, bears are becoming a 'nuisance' in many areas. Constant contact with humans reduces their fear, and they come into towns and homes to search for food. In **national parks** in the USA, bear-proof rubbish bins are provided to stop the bears coming to search for food.

In northern Canada, a female polar bear plods along, with her two half-grown cubs following behind. They don't seem to mind that they are being watched by interested tourists in the vehicles in the background.

These Asian black bear cubs are behind bars, but not for doing anything wrong. If they had not been rescued from their human captors they would have been killed for food and some parts of their bodies would have been used in traditional medicine.

Campers are encouraged not to leave food in tents but to hang it high in a tree, to keep it out of reach.

One good thing to come from bears' acceptance of humans is that more people get a chance to see bears in the wild. Thousands of tourists visit the town of Churchill in northern Canada to see the polar bears that gather together there each year. Special bear-proof vehicles have been built so that the tourists can get within just a metre or so of the bears.

In Alaska, watching brown bears as they catch salmon from the rivers has become so popular that the number of people there at any one time has to be controlled.

## ILLEGAL MEDICINES

In parts of Asia, bears are killed in order to use parts of their bodies in traditional medicines.

The most important part is the animal's gall bladder because it contains bile (a liquid substance made in the liver), which is used as a medicine. Often a bear is killed, in order for the gall bladder to be removed. In some Asian countries, bears are specially **bred** for their bile. These bears are held captive in cramped, unhealthy conditions.

# Conservation

Five of the eight species of bear are in danger of becoming extinct in the near future, unless steps are taken to protect and conserve them.

Only four species of bear are actively protected in the wild. Of these, the American black, the brown and the polar bear are reasonably safe, but the panda is still in great danger of becoming extinct.

Efforts are being made to protect the spectacled bear in South America, but there is little money available to help this project in less developed countries.

Because not much is known about the sun bear, there has been little interest in conserving it, though some research on this species is now being done in Borneo.

So how many bears are left in the world today? The American black bear has the largest population with between 400,000 and 500,000 bears. This is followed by the brown bear, with about 50,000 in North America and 70,000 in Europe and Asia combined. Polar bears are not easy to count, because of their **remote habitat**. There are somewhere between 5000 and 12,000 polar bears left. There are fewer than 10,000 sloth bears, and an unknown number of sun bears, so both **species** are thought to be **endangered**. This is also true of the Asiatic black bear, for which there are no numbers available. At the bottom of the list is the spectacled bear, of which there are less than 2000 in the wild, and the panda,

People are beginning to realize that unless something is done about it, there will soon be no bears left in the wild. However, the grizzly bear now lives in safety in the vast national parks that have been set up in the USA and Canada.

# The teddy bear

The term 'teddy bear' began with US President Theodore 'Teddy' Roosevelt. President Roosevelt – who enjoyed outdoor activities – was invited on a bear hunt in the Mississippi Delta in November 1902. His hosts captured a bear and tied it to a tree, then encouraged

Roosevelt to shoot it. The president thought this was unfair and cowardly and refused. This event was soon the subject of a newspaper cartoon and it attracted attention across the USA. Businesses quickly began making stuffed bears. These new toys became popular and were called 'teddy bears' in honour of the president.

with only around 1000 in the wild. Unless steps are taken to **conserve** bear habitats and protect bears from poaching (illegal hunting), the world may lose some of these extraordinary creatures forever.

Many people know about the work being done in China and in zoos around the world to protect the panda. What is being done for other bears? In 1965, the countries where polar bears live came to an agreement on how the polar bear

should be protected. Most other species of bear have some form of protection, even if this is only in limited areas inside **national parks** or **nature reserves**.

The only real way to protect bears is to teach people more about these interesting animals and to show them how valuable bears are to our world. Because many bears now live in areas that people want for their own living space, this will not be an easy task!

# Glossary

**ancestor**  animal or person that lived long ago, from whom present-day animals are descended

**bred**  kept for reproduction. Animals kept by humans so that they will produce offspring, for food, fur or medicine for example, have been bred.

**canines**  long, pointed teeth at the front of the mouth

**carnassial**  describes the cheek teeth of carnivores, which have a sharp, cutting ridge for slicing up meat

**carnivore**  animal that eats meat

**conservation**  looking after animals and the places they live in order to stop them from becoming extinct

**den**  cosy hiding place, such as a cave, where mother bears give birth to their cubs and some species of bear spend the cold winter months

**endangered**  likely to become extinct in the wild in the near future

**evolve**  change gradually over a very long period of time

**extinct**  when a species of animal no longer exists because they have all died out

**fossil**  remain of a living thing that has been preserved in rock

**groom**  take care of an animal's skin or fur

**habitat**  type of place, or environment, that suits specific plants or animals

**hibernation**  state of very deep sleep in which some animals pass the cold months of winter

**identify**  recognize

**mammal**  animals with fur or hair, whose young feed on milk produced by the mother

**molar**  back tooth with rounded or flattened surface, used for grinding food

**mate** (verb)  joining together of a male and female to produce young (offspring)

**muzzle**  front of a bear's face (sometimes called the snout)

**national park**  area important for its wildlife or scenery that is protected by a country's government

**nature reserve**  area where animals, plants and their habitat are preserved

**nocturnal**  describing animals that are active at night

**omnivore**  animal that eats both animals (meat) and plants

**predator**  animal that catches and eats other animals

**prey**  animal that is caught and eaten by another animal

**remote**  far from areas where lots of people live

**scavenge**  look for scraps of food and left-overs

**spawn**  lay eggs

**species**  name given to describe a particular kind, or type, of animal

**termite**  wood-eating insect that lives in huge colonies, usually in the tropics

**tropics**  hot regions near to the equator, where plants grow all year round

**typical**  having features similar to others of its kind

**ursine**  (bear-like) describes the group to which most bears belong, except for the panda and spectacled bear

**water-resistant**  able to stop water from getting through

**worship**  consider something to be god-like or deserving great respect

# Further information

## Books

*Animal Watch: A Visual Introduction to Bears*, Bernard Stonehouse (Cherrytree Books, 2002)

*Natural World: Grizzly Bear*, Michael Leach (Hodder Wayland, 2000)

*Natural World: Polar Bear*, Malcolm Penny (Hodder Wayland, 1999)

*Nature Watch: Bears and Pandas*, Michael Bright (Lorenz Books, 2000)

## Websites

www.bears.org

www.enchantedlearning.com : search for 'bears'

www.enchantedlearning.com : search for 'pandas'

www.bbc.co.uk/nature/wildfacts : search for 'bears'

www.yahooligans.com : search for 'bears'

www.panda.org : the World Wide Fund for Nature's website

### Disclaimer

All the Internet addresses (URLs) given in this book were valid at the time of going to press. However, due to the dynamic nature of the Internet, some addresses may have changed, or sites may have ceased to exist since publication. While the author and publishers regret any inconvenience this may cause readers, no responsibility for any such changes can be accepted by either the author or the publishers.

# Index

Numbers in *italic* indicate pictures

# Titles in the Secret World of series include:

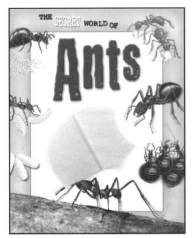

Hardback     1 844 21583 0

Hardback     1 844 21584 9

Hardback     1 844 21588 1

Hardback     1 844 21585 7

Hardback     1 844 21589 X

Hardback     1 844 21590 3

Hardback     1 844 21586 5

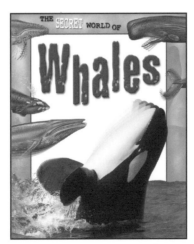

Hardback     1 844 21591 1

Find out about the other titles in this series on our website www.raintreepublishers.co.uk